QUBITS AND QUIVER TREES

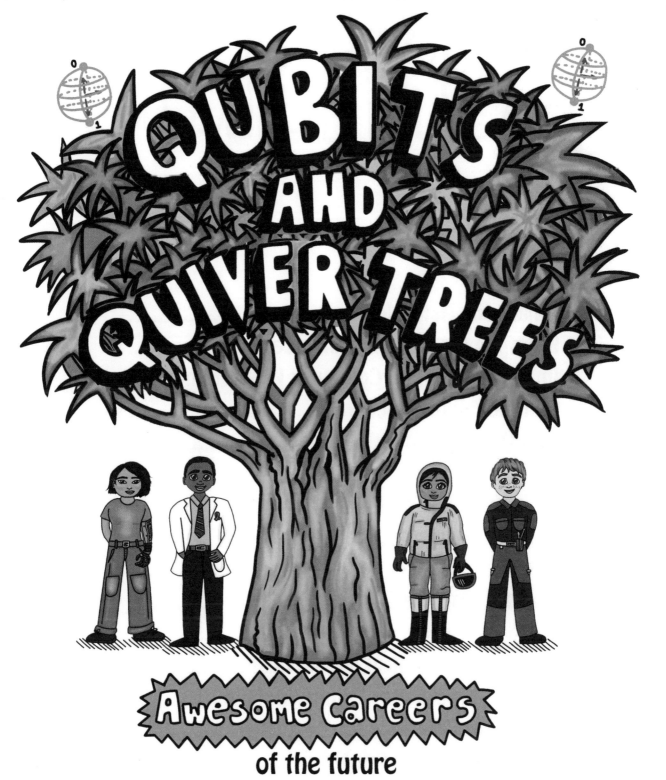

QUBITS AND QUIVER TREES

Awesome Careers

of the future

WRITTEN BY
Bryony Mathew

ILLUSTRATED BY
Millie Bicknelle

CONTENTS

Introduction

The world is changing rapidly. Many children in primary school today will one day take on careers that don't even exist yet. With advances in quantum computing, robotics, nanotechnology and space travel, new opportunities will open up that we can't even imagine.

Qubits and Quiver Trees introduces children to what will be some of the most interesting and important careers over the next 20 years. The book is split into "Qubit Jobs" which look at future discoveries and harnessing new technologies, and "Quiver Tree Jobs" which focus on looking after what we already have and preserving planet Earth for future generations. Both are equally important.

Qubits and Quiver Trees also teaches children that everyone is equal. Children as young as five think people who look less similar to themselves are less kind, and that girls aren't as clever as boys. This book aims to break down those stereotypes and show children that anyone can do anything. It doesn't matter what race, gender or religion someone is, or what abilities, sexual preferences, body shape or medical conditions they have: everyone is equal.

I hope Qubits and Quiver Trees inspires children to learn more about the huge opportunities that await them. I hope it fills them with ideas and energy, builds their confidence, and gets them to believe they can do anything they want to do. The future is theirs.

Bryony Mathew

Qubit Jobs

Future discoveries and harnessing new technologies

AMAYA the ASTEROID MINER

Asteroids are chunks of rock and metal that float in outer space. They are shaped like lumpy potatoes. Most asteroids move around (orbit) the sun in the asteroid belt, which is a ring of space between Mars and Jupiter where millions of asteroids spin and tumble.

Asteroids will be really important in the future because they are full of important materials that we need to make things on Earth, particularly electronic things. Asteroids contain materials like gold, silver, platinum, tungsten, cobalt, titanium, and aluminium. Amaya's job is to take these materials out of asteroids and transport them back to Earth.

She uses special robots called asteroid bots, which she controls with her computer. Amaya can fly these asteroid bots into outer space, land them on asteroids, get them to dig out important materials, and then fly them back to Earth.

Do you like . . .

- ☐ Trying to name all the planets in the right order?
- ☐ Digging for buried treasure?
- ☐ Spinning round and round on a roundabout until you get so dizzy you fall off?

then you might like to be an asteroid miner!

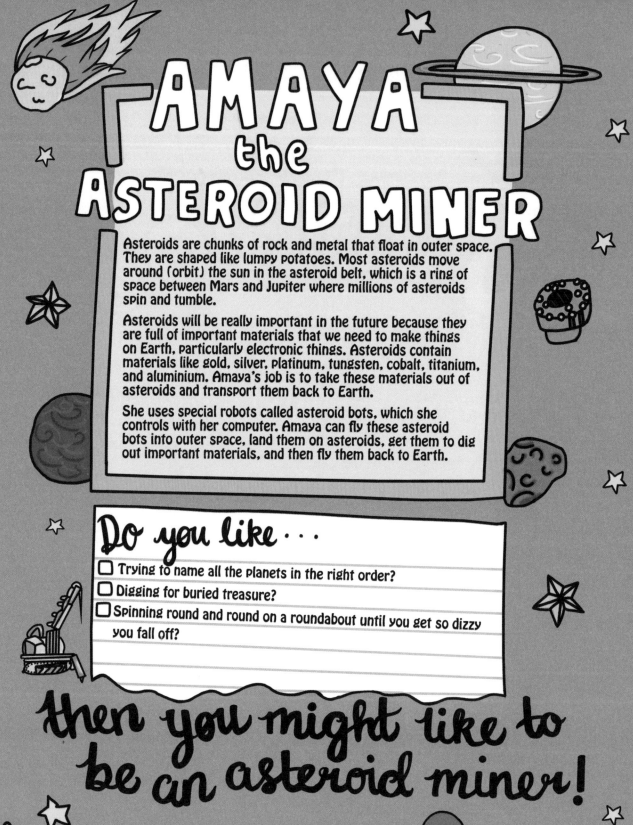

DID YOU KNOW?

Asteroids can be as small as 10m wide or as big as hundreds of kilometres wide! Some asteroids are so big that they are called minor planets. The four biggest asteroids are Ceres, Vesta, Pallas, and Hygiea.

WHERE DO THEY WORK?

Asteroid miners can work at ground stations and space stations, or in workshops, laboratories, or businesses.

BRAM the MECHATRONIC ENGINEER

Bram makes machines that can do complicated tasks. Imagine if your toys could tidy themselves away when you've finished playing with them, or if bins could empty themselves when they get full. The machines that mechatronic engineers make can do these sorts of things.

Bram is good at physics and building things. He can design new machines that can move on their own using electricity. Mechatronic engineers like Bram need to be creative and come up with ideas for new machines that will make people's lives easier. What kind of machine would make your life easier? How about a machine that made your bed? Or a machine that had your favourite snack waiting for you as soon as you got home from school?

Do you like...

☐ Opening up the back of a watch to see how it works?

☐ Turning light switches on and off over and over again?

☐ Using screwdrivers and spanners to put things together?

then you might like to be a mechatronic engineer!

DID YOU KNOW?

The word mechatronic is a mixture of the word mechanic and electronic.

WHERE DO THEY WORK?

Mechatronic engineers can work in laboratories, processing plants and engineering offices.

IMAN
the
QUANTUM COMPUTER
PROGRAMMER

Iman works with quantum computers. These supercomputers are so powerful that they can help us solve tricky problems that normal computers aren't good enough to solve.

Quantum computers are so powerful because they use tiny particles in a very clever way. Normal computers use information called "bits" which can be either 1 or 0 (like being either on or off). But quantum computers use special bits called "qubits" which are very, very tiny. Qubits are special because they can be 1 and 0 at the same time. This is a bit tricky to understand, but what it means is that quantum computers can do more things at the same time. They can run faster than normal computers and still use less energy.

Iman uses her quantum computer to find very big numbers that can be used to keep secrets safe. She can also use it to design new medicines.

Do you like...
☐ Playing on computers?
☐ Coding?
☐ Typing out the longest number you can think of on a calculator?

then you might like to be a quantum computer programmer!

DID YOU KNOW?

Quantum computers are very new. They are still actually being developed. So if you decide to be a quantum computer programmer, you could help build a whole new area of work!

6

WHERE DO THEY WORK?

Quantum computer programmers usually work on computers either in offices or at home.

As long as they have access to computers, they can work just about anywhere!

0

1

5

?

RAFI the COBOT MATCHER

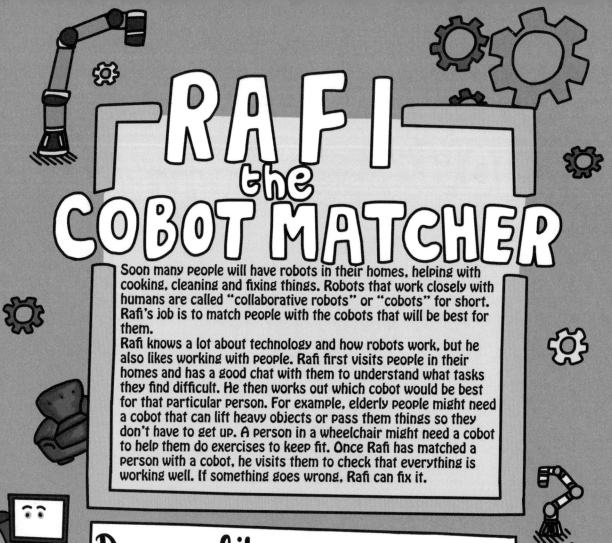

Soon many people will have robots in their homes, helping with cooking, cleaning and fixing things. Robots that work closely with humans are called "collaborative robots" or "cobots" for short. Rafi's job is to match people with the cobots that will be best for them.

Rafi knows a lot about technology and how robots work, but he also likes working with people. Rafi first visits people in their homes and has a good chat with them to understand what tasks they find difficult. He then works out which cobot would be best for that particular person. For example, elderly people might need a cobot that can lift heavy objects or pass them things so they don't have to get up. A person in a wheelchair might need a cobot to help them do exercises to keep fit. Once Rafi has matched a person with a cobot, he visits them to check that everything is working well. If something goes wrong, Rafi can fix it.

Do you like ...

☐ Pretending to be a robot?

☐ Helping people?

☐ Imagining what it would be like if a robot brought you breakfast in bed?

then you might like to be a cobot matcher!

16

DID YOU KNOW?

Cobots are smarter than normal robots.

They are usually also smaller and faster.

WHERE DO THEY WORK?

Cobot matchers spend some of their time visiting people in their homes and some of their time in offices.

17

ELVA the EXPLORATION GEOLOGIST

Elva is a treasure hunter. Her job is to find out where natural resources like gold, minerals, oil and gas are hidden around the world. Elva uses special tests to discover these resources. Sometimes she uses big magnets. Sometimes she measures waves of energy called seismic waves.

Elva is really good at using drills. She drills deep down into the earth and collects different pieces of rock. She then runs tests on the rocks to find out what they're made of and whether they contain any important materials.
Elva uses special computer programs to map out her discoveries and show where natural resources can be found all around the world.

Do you like...

- ☐ Using a metal detector to search for hidden treasure?
- ☐ Digging holes at the beach?
- ☐ Collecting rocks?

then you might like to be an exploration geologist!

DID YOU KNOW?

The outside layer of the Earth is called the crust. Underneath, there is hot liquid rock called magma.

WHERE DO THEY WORK?

Exploration geologists spend much of their time travelling to new places around the world to uncover natural resources. They spend some time on computers, but they spend a lot of their time outside.

ETHAN the SPACE NURSE

Ethan is a nurse who looks after astronauts. Before the astronauts blast off into space, Ethan does lots of tests to make sure they are fit and healthy. He gives astronauts special technologies to wear while they're in space so he can keep a check on things like their heart rate, blood oxygen levels, skin temperature and breathing rate. He also helps them make sure they have all the medicine they will need while they are away from Earth.

While astronauts are in space, Ethan can speak to them. He is there to help answer questions or give them instructions if they have health problems or emergencies. For example, an astronaut might break a bone, cut themselves, or have really bad stomach flu. It is Ethan's job to help make them better. When astronauts land back on Earth again, Ethan is there waiting to check them over and make sure they are healthy after their journey into space.

Do you like...

- ☐ Wondering what it would feel like to float around in space?
- ☐ Sticking on a plaster when you graze your knee?
- ☐ Measuring how tall you are?

then you might like to be a space nurse!

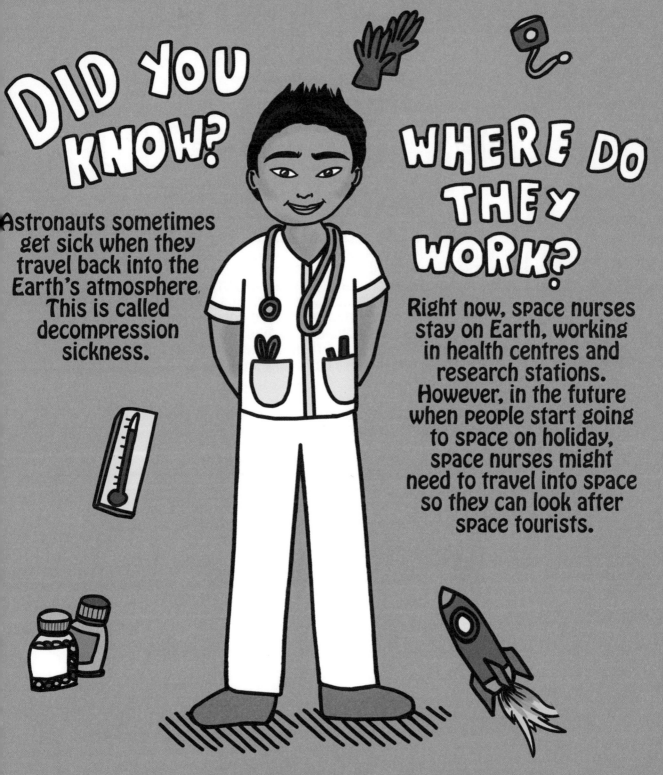

DID YOU KNOW?

Astronauts sometimes get sick when they travel back into the Earth's atmosphere. This is called decompression sickness.

WHERE DO THEY WORK?

Right now, space nurses stay on Earth, working in health centres and research stations. However, in the future when people start going to space on holiday, space nurses might need to travel into space so they can look after space tourists.

NELLA
the CYBER INCIDENT RESPONDER

Nella's job is to keep secret information safe on computers. She is a bit like a firefighter for computer networks. Cyber incident responders like Nella are called whenever a computer network is damaged or there is unauthorised access, which means someone is trying to look at information they're not allowed to see. Nella can use her computer to find problems, work out why they happened, and then fix them to make sure they never happen again. That's how she keeps information safe.

Imagine if a chocolate factory came up with an amazing new recipe, but then someone tried to get into the factory's computers to steal the recipe. Nella would be able to use her own computer to stop them.

Do you like ...

☐ Making up passwords?
☐ Keeping secrets?
☐ Learning new computer languages like Java and Python?

then you might like to be a cyber incident responder!

DID YOU KNOW?

There are lots of other cyber careers that will also be really important in the future, like cyber security administrator, cyber security specialist, cyber security engineer and cryptographer.

WHERE DO THEY WORK?

Cyber incident responders spend most of their time working on computers in offices or in their homes. They usually work for businesses or governments, but they can work for anyone who uses computer networks to store information.

NED the AUGMENTED REALITY ARCHITECT

Augmented reality is technology that makes the real world more exciting. It lets you see real objects and images from a computer at the same time, which makes it look as if computer images are real. Ned's job is to use this technology to design interesting new ways for people to see the world.

Ned can show people what cities would look like with sky trains or flying cars in them. He can show people how they would look in different outfits without having to try them on. Ned can make glasses that help make sure you don't get lost: when you look through the glasses, you see an arrow that points in the direction you should go. He can also do fun things like fill your vision with penguins or ice creams so that you feel as though you're surrounded by your favourite things!

Do you like ...

- ☐ Virtual reality?
- ☐ Wearing special glasses to watch 3D films?
- ☐ Playing computer games?

then you might like to be an augmented reality architect

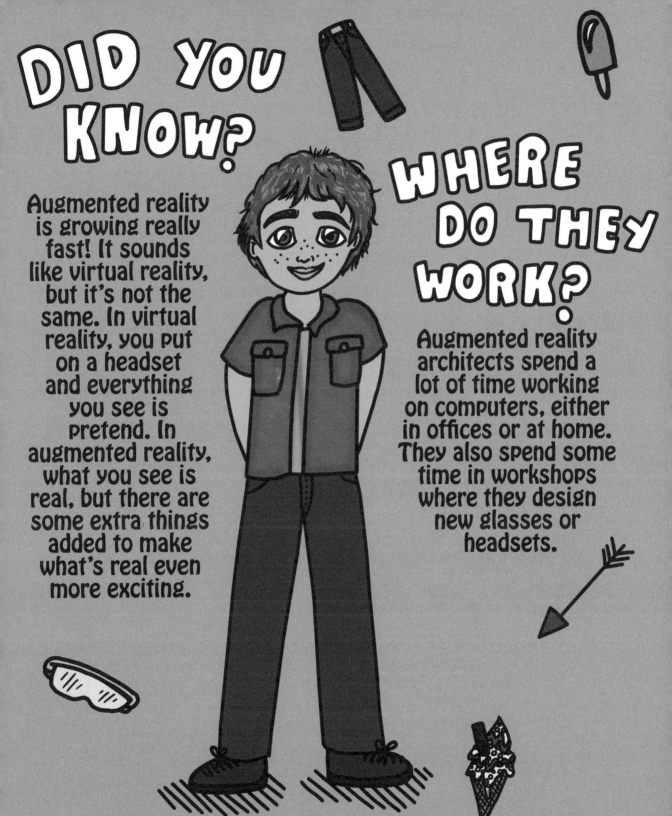

DID YOU KNOW?

Augmented reality is growing really fast! It sounds like virtual reality, but it's not the same. In virtual reality, you put on a headset and everything you see is pretend. In augmented reality, what you see is real, but there are some extra things added to make what's real even more exciting.

WHERE DO THEY WORK?

Augmented reality architects spend a lot of time working on computers, either in offices or at home. They also spend some time in workshops where they design new glasses or headsets.

AYESHA the SPACECRAFT OPERATOR

Ayesha's job is to make sure that spacecraft work well. A spacecraft is a vehicle that can travel into space and back to Earth again. They usually take off from launch pads at special airports called spaceports.

Some spacecraft carry people. Some are satellites which can do things like take pictures of Earth from far away in space. Some satellites bounce back TV and phone signals to Earth. Others help us predict the weather.

Spacecraft operators like Ayesha are good at engineering. Before a mission to space, Ayesha gets the spacecraft ready and makes sure all the different parts are working properly. After the spacecraft has launched and is travelling up in space, she studies the information that it sends back to make sure everything is all right. When a spacecraft returns to Earth, Ayesha checks to see which parts need fixing. If there is a problem, she knows how to fix it. Ayesha makes sure the spacecraft is ready to go for the next mission.

Do you like ...

☐ Counting down 3,2,1 and then pretending to blast off into space?
☐ Using a screwdriver to fix things?
☐ Climbing into a cardboard box and pretending you're in a space rocket?

then you might like to be a spacecraft operator!

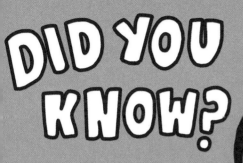

DID YOU KNOW?

Apart from Earth, the only place people have stepped on in space is the Moon. But we have sent machines to investigate Mars, Saturn, Jupiter, and many other far-away places. In the future, people want to be able to visit other planets - if you become a spacecraft operator, maybe you could help them!

WHERE DO THEY WORK?

Spacecraft operators usually work at ground stations or spaceports. When a spacecraft is back on Earth, spacecraft operators work inside spacecraft. They spend a lot of time in the orbiter crew module, which is the part of the spacecraft where astronauts live when they are in space.

JAALI
the
MACHINE LEARNING
ENGINEER

Jaali makes smart computers. His job is to teach computers to think and learn like humans do. This is called machine learning or artificial intelligence (AI). Jaali can make machines that can understand speech, recognise people's faces or even tell people what illness they have.

Jaali is really good at maths and at computer programming. He feeds lots of information into computers and programs them so they can make decisions and predictions about what will happen in the future. With Jaali's help, smart computers can learn to do things without being told exactly what to do. For example, Jaali can make toys that talk back when children speak to them. To do this, Jaali needs to give the computer inside the toy lots of information: different types of voices, different things children say and different responses. Then he programs the toys so they always choose the best response when a child talks to them.

Do you like...

☐ Wondering what's inside your own head?

☐ Computer programming?

☐ Imagining what it would be like if you weren't feeling well and your computer could tell you what was wrong?

then you might like to be a machine learning engineer!

DID YOU KNOW?

Machine learning engineers need to know different computer programming languages like Python, R, Lisp, and Prolog.

WHERE DO THEY WORK?

Machine learning engineers work in workshops, offices, laboratories and universities.

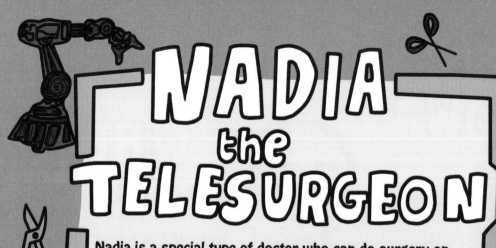

NADIA the TELESURGEON

Nadia is a special type of doctor who can do surgery on someone even if they're far away. She uses robots and special video systems to operate on people who can't easily get to a doctor.

To perform surgery in a hard-to-reach place, first Nadia gets a drone to fly into the area and drop off a special telesurgery kit with robotic arms, cameras and surgical tools. Nadia can then operate using these robotic arms - she can fix people even though she's not there with them!

Telesurgery is particularly useful in emergency situations like when a soldier gets injured in a battle, when someone hurts themselves while they're climbing a mountain or when someone lives far away from a hospital. In these cases, it's much easier to fly a drone in and drop off a telesurgery kit than for the patient to get to a doctor.

Do you like...

- ☐ Using grab sticks to pick things up?
- ☐ Very carefully cutting out a tricky shape using scissors?
- ☐ Playing with remote control cars?

then you might like to be a telesurgeon!

DID YOU KNOW?

New technology could make telesurgery even smoother than normal surgery because it could make small problems go away, like the small shakes of a surgeon's hand.

WHERE DO THEY WORK?

Telesurgeons work in special telesurgical units. These are rooms with computers, video screens and robots that are linked to operating rooms or to cameras far away.

DEEPAK
the
TECHNICAL AGRONOMIST

Deepak uses new technology to help farmers produce more food and better food. He uses drones to fly over fields so he can see how crops are growing. He helps design machines that can plant seeds in exactly the right places. He also creates machines that can identify which plants are sick and spray them to make them better.

Deepak also helps design robotic feeders that feed farm animals automatically so farmers don't have to get up before sunrise. Those machines also mean animals get exactly the right amount of food. By using technology like this, Deepak saves the farmer money and time.

Do you like ...

☐ Planting vegetables and eating them when they're ready?

☐ Riding in a tractor?

☐ Jumping in sprinklers that are watering the garden?

then you might like to be a technical agronomist!

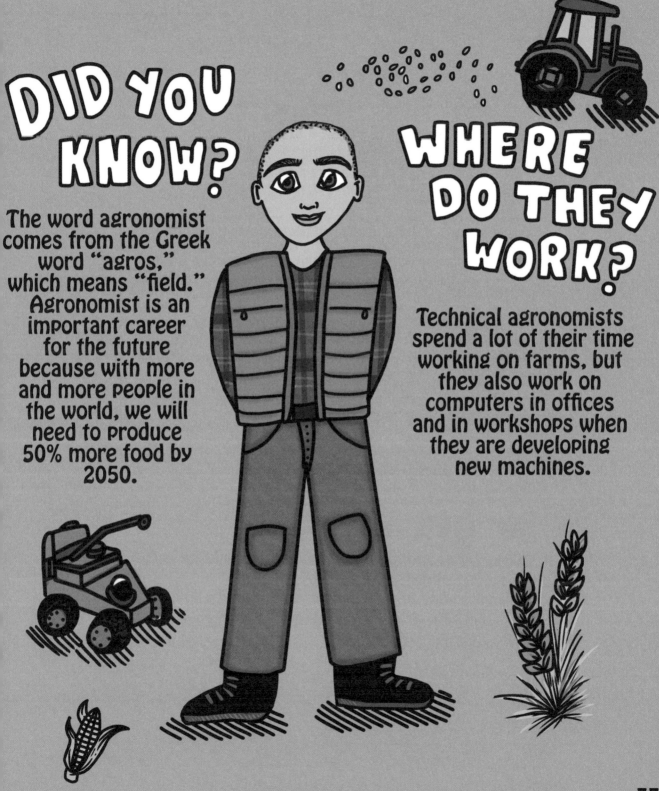

DID YOU KNOW?

The word agronomist comes from the Greek word "agros," which means "field." Agronomist is an important career for the future because with more and more people in the world, we will need to produce 50% more food by 2050.

WHERE DO THEY WORK?

Technical agronomists spend a lot of their time working on farms, but they also work on computers in offices and in workshops when they are developing new machines.

SOFIA the INTERNET OF THINGS ARCHITECT

Imagine if objects could talk to you — wouldn't that be fun? What if the fridge could tell you when it's running out of milk? Or your watch could send a message to the front door so that the door swings open as soon as you arrive home? An Internet of Things architect like Sofia can make that happen.

Sofia designs new ways to make objects smart so they can communicate with you and with each other. These talking objects are called The Internet of Things because they are all things that are connected by the internet. You can control them through an app on a phone or your watch. If you were an Internet of Things architect, what would you want your objects to do?

Do you like ...

☐ Wondering what it would be like if your pens could tell you how to do your homework?
☐ Wearing a watch that counts how many steps you take?
☐ Imagining what it would be like if your school bag could tell you what to pack each day?

then you might like to be an internet of things architect!

34

DID YOU KNOW?

The Internet of Things is growing very quickly. Soon even cars and clothes will be connected to the internet!

WHERE DO THEY WORK?

Internet of Things architects spend a lot of their time working on computers in offices or in their homes. They work for companies, research centres and governments.

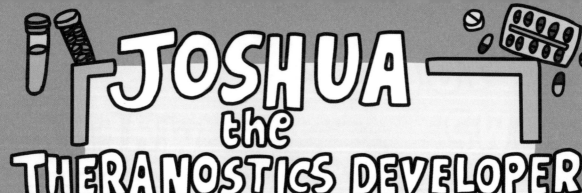

JOSHUA the THERANOSTICS DEVELOPER

Joshua's job is to find new ways to fix people when they get sick. Normally, everyone who gets the same illness gets the same medicine. But Joshua thinks people should have medicine designed especially for them. That way, the medicine will work better.

Joshua works in a new type of science called theranostics. He uses a scanner to look inside people's bodies. Then he sends medicine to exactly where it needs to go using tiny little robots called nanobots. Joshua watches on his computer so he can see when the nanobot reaches the sick part of the body and make sure it does exactly what it needs to do to fix the illness. Sometimes the nanobots need to release more medicine; sometimes they need to release less. Sometimes Joshua can see that the medicine isn't working, so he changes it for a different type of medicine that will work better for that particular person. In the future, theranostics will hopefully be able to help doctors treat serious illnesses like cancer and heart disease.

Do you like ...

☐ Using a syringe to measure tiny amounts of medicine?
☐ Trying to balance a see-saw?
☐ Playing with magnets?

then you might like to be a theranostics developer!

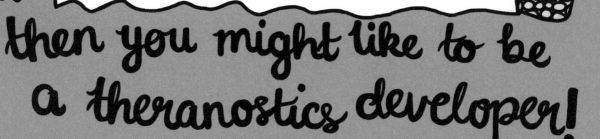

DID YOU KNOW?

The word "theranostics" is a mixture of the words "therapy" (which means treatment) and "diagnostics" (which means identification), so theranostics is when you identify and treat an illness at the same time. It's a new, exciting area of science.

WHERE DO THEY WORK?

Theranostics developers work in laboratories and hospitals. They know about physics, chemistry and nanotechnology, and they spend a lot of their time using computers and scanners.

LUCIA
the
3D FOOD PRINTER

Lucia's job is to print food! Normally, food comes straight from animals or plants, but Lucia can print food with a special 3D printer, using things like powders containing essential nutrients. Printing food is important because there are so many people in the world, and we need to find ways to make sure there is enough food for everyone to eat.

3D food printer engineers like Lucia can also help with space travel! When humans are able to travel to Mars, that journey will take a very long time. It will probably be difficult to take fresh food with them because it won't be able to last. But if astronauts can print food while they're in their spaceship, they will be able to travel even further away and explore new planets.

Do you like...

☐ Trying new food you've never tasted before?

☐ Decorating cakes with as much icing and sprinkles as you can fit?

☐ Coming up with crazy combinations of sandwich fillings like peanut butter, sausage and strawberries?

then you might like to be a 3D food printer!

DID YOU KNOW?

By the year 2050, there will be 9 billion people in the world, and our farms won't be able to produce enough food to feed everyone. That means we need to find other creative ways of getting food, like 3D printing.

WHERE DO THEY WORK?

3D food printer engineers normally work in laboratories, workshops and offices. Some work in space agencies, studying how to print food in outer space.

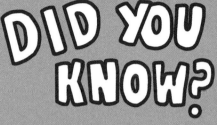

ALEX the ASTROBIOLOGIST

Alex's job is to find out whether there are any plants or creatures living on other planets. He even tries to find out whether aliens exist!

Astrobiologists like Alex try to understand what life needs in order to survive in many different types of environment. To do this, Alex studies other planets to see whether the environment makes it safe for something to live there. He also spends a lot of time in laboratories testing whether bacteria can survive in difficult environments. Sometimes he looks at fossils and tries to work out how they got to be on planet Earth.

To find out whether there might be aliens somewhere out there, Alex searches for radio signals from other intelligent life in the universe.

Do you like ...

☐ Imagining what it would be like to live on Mars?
☐ Looking up at the night sky to see if you can spot a flying saucer?
☐ Imagining what you'd say to an alien if a spaceship landed in your garden?

then you might like to be an astrobiologist!

DID YOU KNOW?

An astrobiologist is usually an expert in biology as well as in astronomy.

WHERE DO THEY WORK?

Astrobiologists usually work in universities or research institutions.

AZAMI the NANOROBOTICS ENGINEER

Azami is a nanorobotics engineer. Her job is to build really tiny robots called nanorobots (or nanobots for short). Nanobots can move the smallest things in the world (atoms) around and build things out of them. Everything you can see around you is made up of atoms, but they are so small that you need a really strong microscope to be able to see them.

Nanobots can get to places that normal robots can't reach, like inside the human body. They can deliver medicine to exactly the right part of the body, and they can find bad things inside the body like cancer cells and destroy them. They can also check our health and send a message to let us know when there is a problem somewhere inside the body.

Nanorobotics is still quite new, so if you decide to become a nanorobotics engineer, you could help design all sorts of new ways that tiny robots could make people's lives better.

Do you like ...

☐ Imagining what it would be like if you could shrink to the size of an ant?

☐ Looking at tiny things through a microscope?

☐ Using tweezers to pick up tiny little beads?

then you might like to be nanorobotics engineer!

DID YOU KNOW?

The word nano means really, really small. One nanometre is one billionth of a metre. That is a million times smaller than the length of an ant!

WHERE DO THEY WORK?

Nanorobotics engineers work in workshops and laboratories. They spend a lot of time using microscopes.

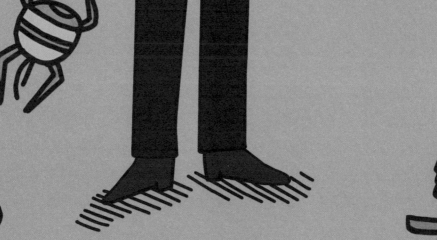

Quiver Tree Jobs

Looking after what we already have and preserving planet Earth for future generations

ARRTU the FORESTER

Arrtu's job is to protect forests. This is a really important job because forests make oxygen, which we need to breathe. Forests also provide us with food, medicine and fuel, and they are home to lots of amazing animals and plants. A long time ago, before we started to build big cities, more than half of the Earth was covered in forests. Now less than 10% of those forests are left.

In many places around the world, forests are being cut down so that the trees can be made into paper or furniture, or used as fuel to heat buildings. In some places, whole forests are being cleared so the land can be used for building houses or to make space for cattle. This is called deforestation. Deforestation is bad for the world because trees help stop climate change by trapping gases produced by human activity.

Arrtu spends a lot of time outside in the forest, exploring nature, planting new trees, checking for fire risks, and sometimes even fighting forest fires. He also visits schools to teach children about how to help look after our forests.

Do you like ...

☐ Playing outside?
☐ Planting apple seeds and watching them grow into apple trees?
☐ Climbing trees?

then you might like to be a forester!

DID YOU KNOW?

Up to 7 billion trees are being cut down every year. If we carry on destroying forests at this rate, there won't be any tropical rainforests left in the world in 100 years.

WHERE DO THEY WORK?

Foresters spend most of their time outdoors in forests. They wrap up warm in cold weather and don't mind being outside in the rain. When they need to work on a computer, foresters work inside, either at home or in an office.

ZAYNAH the POLAR SCIENTIST

Zaynah's job is to explore the coldest places in the world. She goes on expeditions to the North and South Poles to make discoveries and study how the Earth works. Zaynah collects information about icebergs, ice mountains and plants. She also studies polar animals. Some animals only live in the North Pole, like polar bears and walruses. Some animals only live in the South Pole, like penguins and leopard seals.

Sometimes Zaynah spends a whole summer living in the South Pole. She spends her time tracking animals, looking for plants, and taking measurements of things like sea level and sea ice thickness. She looks for patterns so that she can predict what might happen in the future. Zaynah also studies the effects of climate change. She uses computer models to help her to answer questions like, "What will happen if the Earth gets warmer and icebergs melt into the sea?"

Do you like...

☐ Building igloos?
☐ Imagining what it would be like to go all the way to the North Pole?
☐ Having snowball fights?

then you might like to be a polar scientist!

DID YOU KNOW?

The area around the North Pole is called the Arctic and the area around the South Pole is called the Antarctic.

WHERE DO THEY WORK?

Polar scientists usually spend some of their time working at universities and laboratories and some of their time in the North or South pole living at specially designed research bases, often working with scientists from all around the world.

BEN
the
CLIMATOLOGIST

Ben is a scientist who knows all about weather patterns. He looks at changes that are happening to the weather over a long period of time. This is called the climate.

Climatologists like Ben have discovered that the earth is getting warmer. This is not good for people, plants, or animals. A warmer planet means some places are becoming much hotter and wetter than they used to be, so it's becoming difficult to live there. A warmer planet is also bad for crops. Plants and animals might not be able to survive if it suddenly becomes much too hot or much too cold for them. Some plants, like Quiver Trees in Africa, are already in danger because it's getting too hot for them to survive. If the Earth keeps getting warmer, soon there won't be any Quiver Trees left.

Another really big problem that Ben works on is that the polar ice caps are starting to melt into the sea. This is making the level of the sea higher, which is dangerous because many of the world's big cities are built close to the sea. If those cities flood, millions of people would be affected.

Do you like...

- ☐ Lying on the grass and watching clouds moving above your head?
- ☐ Racing raindrops down the window?
- ☐ On a windy day, holding onto an umbrella as tightly as you can and seeing if you can be blown along?

then you might like to be a climatologist!

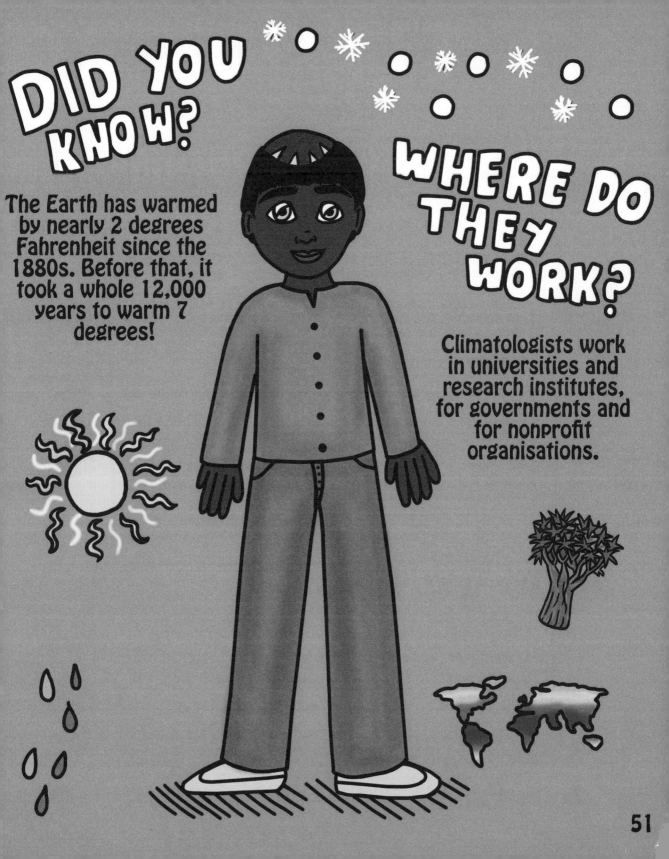

DID YOU KNOW?

The Earth has warmed by nearly 2 degrees Fahrenheit since the 1880s. Before that, it took a whole 12,000 years to warm 7 degrees!

WHERE DO THEY WORK?

Climatologists work in universities and research institutes, for governments and for nonprofit organisations.

51

ELLEN
the
EARTH OBSERVATION
SCIENTIST

Ellen looks at big changes happening in the world with the help of satellites. Satellites travel around the Earth and take pictures and measurements, like temperature. Ellen uses these to research how things are changing, like where forests are being cut down, where buildings are being built, or where sea temperatures are changing. She makes maps that show changes happening on land and in the sea. Ellen can even see how much of the Earth's natural resources are being used up.

By using satellites, Ellen can look at areas of the Earth that are difficult to visit. Sometimes, when there has been a natural disaster like an earthquake or a tsunami, Ellen is called in to look at what damage has been done so that help can be sent to the people living there. New technology is being developed that will allow Ellen to see even more areas of the Earth more clearly and quickly, which will help her to respond to natural disasters faster.

Do you like ...

☐ Looking at pictures of the Earth taken from space and trying to work out where you live?

☐ Drawing maps and carefully marking out all the important places?

☐ Using a camera to take pictures of things far away?

then you might like to be an earth observation scientist

DID YOU KNOW?

There are lots of different types of satellites. Some are for communication, some are for weather and some are for science research. The International Space Station is even a satellite!

WHERE DO THEY WORK?

Earth observation scientists spend a lot of time working on computers. They can work for companies that look at the environment, NGOs, research labs and universities, and even for space agencies.

HAMZA the HYDROLOGIST

Hamza is a water scientist. Hydro means water, and water is one of the most important things in the world because without water, there would be no life on Earth. Although there is a lot of water in the world, much of it is salty sea water that we can't drink or use to water crops. Many people don't have clean water to drink, and soon there won't be enough water for farmers to grow crops. Hydrologists like Hamza need to come up with new ways to save water and get it to the places it is needed most.

Hamza studies all sorts of things about water. He studies how much rain falls from the sky, where it goes after it soaks into the ground and how it returns to the oceans and air. He studies what's in our drinking water and how to make it clean. He also finds new ways to move water from one place to another and can predict what will happen if there are storms, droughts or flooding.

One of the most important things Hamza does is to help make sure people have clean water to drink. He can teach people how to make water safer to drink and how to find water in places where there isn't very much.

Do you like ...

- ☐ Carefully turning on a tap so that just a single drop of water comes out?
- ☐ Swimming in rivers?
- ☐ Listening to the sound of raindrops falling on the roof while you're snuggled up inside?

then you might like to be a hydrologist!

DID YOU KNOW?

Nearly 800 million people don't have clean drinking water right now. By 2025, almost 2 billion people will live in places where there is not enough water. The world needs more hydrologists to find ways to fix this huge problem.

WHERE DO THEY WORK?

Hydrologists spend a lot of time outside gathering information, collecting water and soil samples, and speaking to local people. They also spend time in offices, working on computers to study the information they've collected.

YING-YUE
the REWILDER

Ying Yue's job is to bring back nature. She is like a magician who can turn old ruined pieces of land into beautiful gardens, parks, and forests. First Ying Yue needs to make a plan for how she wants the land to look. She uses computers to produce virtual pictures showing where different types of plants and trees will go and where there will be hills or planted gardens. Sometimes she brings back wetlands and sometimes she brings back forests. She can even change the direction of small rivers if she needs to.

Once Ying Yue knows how she wants the area to look, she needs to clear the land. She works with a team of people to take down any buildings and get rid of rubbish before she brings in new soil and rocks and starts planting trees and flowers to turn it into a lovely, natural place.

Do you like ...

☐ Planting seeds and watching them grow?
☐ Watering the garden?
☐ Building mud banks in tiny rivers to try to get the water to flow in different directions?

then you might like to be a rewilder!

DID YOU KNOW?

Some rewilders bring in animals or bugs as well as plants and waterways. These can help the area to grow into a really special, healthy, natural place.

WHERE DO THEY WORK?

Rewilders can work anywhere there is land or water that needs to be turned back into nature. They spend a lot of time outdoors, but they also need to spend some time working on computers while they are coming up with new designs.

KHALID
the
OCEAN CONSERVATIONIST

Khalid's job is to protect the ocean. The ocean is important because it gives us food and water, it controls our weather, it makes some of the air we breathe and it gets rid of some of the gases we don't need. Khalid studies ocean plants and animals. Some of these are endangered, which means they could disappear forever because there aren't many of them left. Hawksbill turtles, angel sharks, monk seals and sea grass are all endangered species, but ocean conservationists like Khalid can help them survive.

Another really important problem that Khalid can help fix is ocean plastic. Our oceans are becoming filled with plastic rubbish, which is very bad for sea creatures. Sometimes they get tangled up in plastic bags and can't get out. Sometimes they eat bits of plastic, which can be very bad for them. The plastics also release nasty chemicals that make it difficult for creatures to survive. Khalid tries to find ways to get rid of this plastic waste. One of the best ways to do this is to teach people to recycle their rubbish and to stop using so much plastic so that there is less waste in the future.

Do you like ...

☐ Swimming in the ocean?
☐ Jumping over waves at the beach?
☐ Saving energy by turning off lights when you go out of a room?

then you might like to be an ocean conservationist!

DID YOU KNOW?

No one knows how many creatures live in the ocean. New creatures are being discovered all the time. There could be as many as 10 million different ocean creatures!

WHERE DO THEY WORK?

Ocean conservationists spend a lot of their time at the ocean, on research ships, or sometimes staying on islands. The rest of their time is spent in laboratories at universities or research institutes.

ROSY the DIPLOMAT

Rosy's job is to keep peace around the world by speaking to people from different countries. If there are disagreements, Rosy knows just how to solve them. She spends a lot of time listening to what people from different countries think and want, and she finds ways for them to work together. Sometimes she helps countries work together to stop climate change. Sometimes she helps them work together to stop wars or famine.

Diplomats like Rosy spend a lot of time living in different countries around the world, and they can usually speak a lot of different languages. Rosy needs to get to know people living in other countries and really understand what it's like to live there. She also helps people when they run into trouble when travelling. If you lose your passport or have an accident when you're on holiday, a diplomat can help you. Really important diplomats are called ambassadors.

Do you like...

☐ Learning to speak different languages?
☐ Passing on secret messages?
☐ Fixing arguments between friends?

then you might like to be a diplomat!

DID YOU KNOW?

The word diplomacy comes from the Greek word diploma which means an object folded in two. This is because many years ago, people were given permission to travel by being given documents folded in two.

WHERE DO THEY WORK?

Diplomats move around a lot. They usually spend three or four years in one country and then they move to another one. When they are in their home country, they work in a government building called a Ministry of Foreign Affairs. When they are abroad, they work in buildings called embassies.

MAX the CLINICAL PSYCHOLOGIST

Max's job is to help people feel happier and to do more of the things they want to do. You know how different parts of your body sometimes get sick, like when you have a stomach ache or a sore throat? Well your mind can get sick too. If your mind is sick, it can be hard for you to do other things, like go to work or meet up with friends and you can feel really sad. A clinical psychologist like Max can help you feel better. He is a bit like a mind doctor, helping people with their mental health.

First Max needs to work out exactly what the problem is. He spends time talking to the patient, asking questions and doing some special tests that help him understand what sorts of thoughts are going on inside the patient's head. Then he can help the patient to look after these thoughts and start to feel happier. Max also does lots of research to try to understand how the mind works so that he can find new ways to help people feel better.

Do you like ...

☐ Wondering how your brain works?
☐ Trying to guess what someone else is thinking?
☐ Cheering up your friends when they're feeling sad?

then you might like to be a clinical psychologist!

DID YOU KNOW?

Clinical psychologists need university degrees, but there are other jobs where you can help people with mental health problems that don't need as much studying, like mental health counsellor, psychiatric technician and mental health nurse.

WHERE DO THEY WORK?

Clinical psychologists can choose to work in hospitals, health centres, schools, prisons and community mental health teams. They can also visit people in their own homes.

MAHIRA the ENTOMOLOGIST

Mahira knows all about insects like bees, ants, beetles and butterflies. She is a scientist who studies how insects behave, what they eat and how they reproduce. Sometimes Mahira looks after insects in laboratories. Sometimes she goes out on expeditions to watch how insects behave in the wild.

One of the most important things Mahira looks at is how insects spread diseases. Mosquitos can spread diseases like malaria and dengue fever. When they bite a sick person, mosquitos can pick up a virus or bacteria. It doesn't make the mosquito feel bad, but the mosquito can pass on the virus or bacteria to the next person it bites. So Mahira needs to find out how to stop mosquitos from being able to carry viruses and bacteria - that way, people won't get sick when they are bitten. There are millions and millions of mosquitos in the world, so entomologists are very important because they can help stop a lot of people getting ill!

Do you like ...

☐ Letting ladybirds land on your hand and counting their spots?
☐ Carefully following a line of ants to see where they're off to?
☐ Watching bees in the garden and guessing which flower they're going to land on next?

then you might like to be an entomologist!

DID YOU KNOW?

There is a special type of entomology called forensic entomology, where scientists use their knowledge of insects to help the police solve crimes.

WHERE DO THEY WORK?

Entomologists work in all sorts of different places, from universities, laboratories and zoos to museums, military agencies and biotechnology companies.

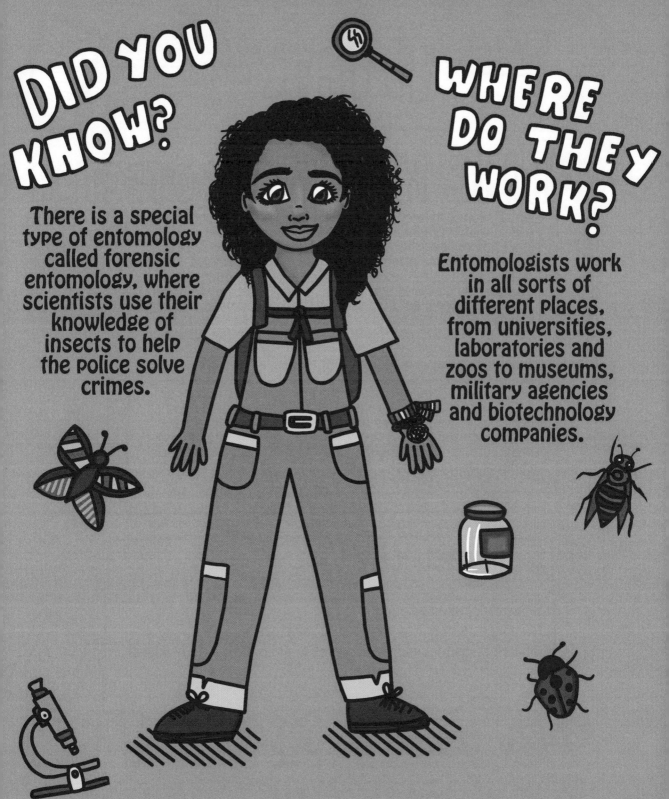

AMAR
the
PUBLIC HEALTH PROTECTOR

Amar's job is to keep people healthy. He studies diseases like the flu that spread quickly and make people feel very sick. Have you noticed that when one person in your class gets sick, other people often get sick, too? This is because diseases can be passed from one person to another. Amar studies how diseases spread. He collects information about how many people get ill, where they get ill and what treatment makes them better. He then uses this information to figure out how to stop more people from getting ill in the future.

Amar is good at making plans. He thinks about what sorts of health emergencies could happen, like the outbreak of a disease like Ebola, or extreme weather like heat waves, or really bad pollution. Amar then helps doctors, nurses and hospitals make sure they are ready to help in case of a big emergency and he tells the public what to do if lots of people start getting sick. Sometimes he tells people to wear special clothing like face masks. Sometimes he tells them to wash their hands or take medicine.

Do you like ...

☐ Playing doctors and nurses?
☐ Writing lists of things you need to remember?
☐ Making plans for what you're going to do in the school holidays?

then you might like to be a public health protector!

DID YOU KNOW?

A big outbreak of a disease is called an epidemic. If an epidemic is so big that it spreads across different continents around the world, then it is called a pandemic.

WHERE DO THEY WORK?

Public health protectors can work in hospitals, health centres, universities, or for the government.

MADELEINE the EARTHQUAKE PREDICTOR

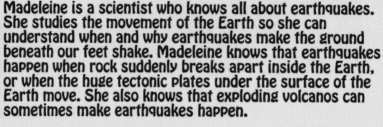

Madeleine is a scientist who knows all about earthquakes. She studies the movement of the Earth so she can understand when and why earthquakes make the ground beneath our feet shake. Madeleine knows that earthquakes happen when rock suddenly breaks apart inside the Earth, or when the huge tectonic plates under the surface of the Earth move. She also knows that exploding volcanos can sometimes make earthquakes happen.

One of the most important things Madeleine does is predict when an earthquake is likely to happen so that people can move to safe places so they don't get hurt. Earthquakes happen most often in countries that are above where two tectonic plates touch, like Indonesia and Japan. These countries make special buildings that can move when the ground shakes. This means the buildings don't fall down and the people inside them stay safe.

Do you like ...

- ☐ Poking a jelly and watching it wobble?
- ☐ Jumping on the bed?
- ☐ Carefully balancing rocks on top of each other to see how big a pile you can make?

then you might like to be an earthquake predictor!

DID YOU KNOW?

Another name for an earthquake scientist is seismologist, because they study the movement of the earth called seismic waves.

WHERE DO THEY WORK?

Earthquake predictors work in universities, research centres, energy companies and government organisations. They can spend a lot of time travelling to different countries around the world where earthquakes happen.

LEO the RECYCLER

Leo's job is to turn things we don't need any more into something new. This is called recycling. Normally, all the waste that you put in the bin gets sent to a big hole in the ground called a landfill. This is very bad for the environment because the waste poisons the Earth. But lots of waste could be recycled instead. Recycling is really important because it saves money, materials and natural resources and means we use fewer landfills. It also means we don't use as much energy, it makes the air and water cleaner and it helps stop climate change.

Recyclers like Leo can melt down glass, metal and plastic and make it into bottles, pens and drinks cans. He can recycle rubbish made of paper and cardboard into kitchen towels and toilet paper. He can even recycle things like clothes, toys and carpets.

Recyclers will be really important in the future. A lot of new technologies depends on rare earth elements that are very expensive to extract. If Leo can find ways to take these elements out of old electronic items, batteries, lasers and ceramics, then they can be used in new types of technology.

Do you like ...

☐ Sorting rubbish into different bins?

☐ Getting into a really bubbly bubble bath and coming out squeaky clean?

☐ Watching candles melt?

then you might like to be a recycler!

DID YOU KNOW?

Whenever you buy food, you can check the wrapper to see whether it can be recycled. There will be little pictures on the back which tell you whether the wrapper can be recycled or not.

WHERE DO THEY WORK?

Recyclers usually work at waste recycling centres or in offices. Sometimes they work in a recycling vehicle that drives around town, collecting rubbish for recycling.

Hidden Differences

Everyone is different, and that's what makes us special.

Everyone has things they have difficulty with, that they're scared of, that they like or don't like.

Some people come from very poor families;
some people are sick;
some people have a dad but no mum, or two mums but
no dad, or no mum or dad.

Our differences don't change the fact that
everyone is equal.

The characters in this book all have hidden differences too.

Turn over to find out more.

Ayesha has two dads. Joshua has a mum but no dad. Ethan doesn't have any parents; he grew up in a care home.

Ned is coeliac. That means that his body can't digest gluten properly, so he can't eat food like bread, pasta, or cakes. They make him feel very ill.

DID YOU

Khalid had to leave his home country because of a war. It wasn't safe for him to stay, so he travelled for three months to get to a safe country.

Amaya was the first person in her family to go to university.

Azami really struggled with maths at school and needed extra lessons.

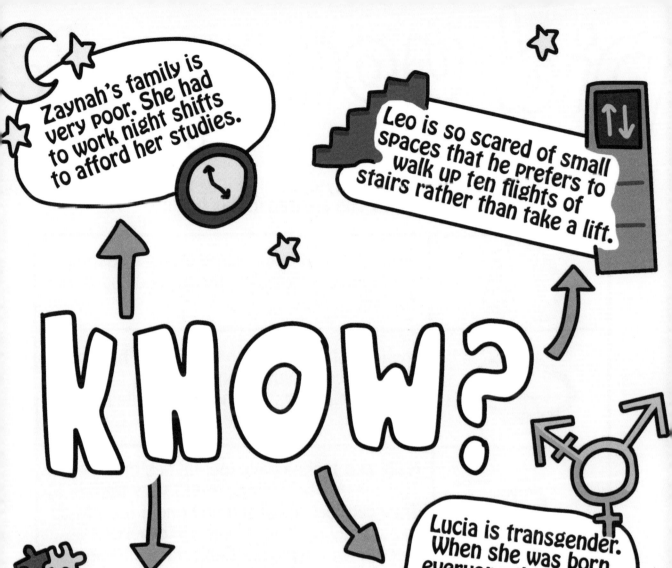

Zaynah's family is very poor. She had to work night shifts to afford her studies.

Leo is so scared of small spaces that he prefers to walk up ten flights of stairs rather than take a lift.

KNOW?

Iman has autism spectrum disorder. She sees, hears, and feels the world differently than other people. Iman finds social interactions uncomfortable and can have difficulty communicating.

Lucia is transgender. When she was born, everyone thought she was a boy, but inside she always knew she was really a girl. So she changed her name and her clothes and started living as a girl.

Did you spot?

Sometimes you can see little signs or symbols that give hints about differences. See how many you spotted in this book:

	Max can't hear well, so he wears a hearing aid in his ear to make sounds loud enough for him to hear.
	Nadia is diabetic, which means she has too much glucose (sugar) in her blood. She has to have injections of a hormone called insulin to keep her blood sugar just right.
	Nella and Joshua have mental health issues. This means their minds aren't very well. They can feel really sad and find it hard to do things they want to do like go to work or meet up with friends. Clinical Psychologists like Max can help them.
	Rafi has epilepsy. That means his brain sometimes suddenly has bursts of activity that give him seizures (fits). During a seizure, Rafi can't control how his body moves.
	Jaali has vitiligo. Vitiligo is a skin condition where patches of skin lose their colour.

	This is an asthma inhaler. Asthma is a health problem that makes it hard to breathe. Hamza uses his inhaler to suck medicine into his lungs to make it easier for him to breathe.
	Madeleine had a type of cancer called a brain tumour when she was young. She was very sick, but then had an operation to take the tumour out. She was lucky that the surgeons managed to take out the whole tumour and now she is all better.
	The rainbow flag is about loving who you want to love. Some boys love boys, some girls love girls, and some people love both boys and girls.
	Mahira has dyslexia, which makes reading, writing, and spelling difficult for her.
	Ying Ye was born without her left arm, so she now has a bionic arm instead.

Despite all these different backgrounds and different challenges and experiences, everyone has managed to get a great job.

We are all different, and that is what makes us special. With the right support and the right treatment for any illnesses, anyone can do anything.

e nice to others. Treat them how you would like to be treated yourself. f you do, then not only will you go on to achieve great things, but most importantly, you will be proud of yourself.

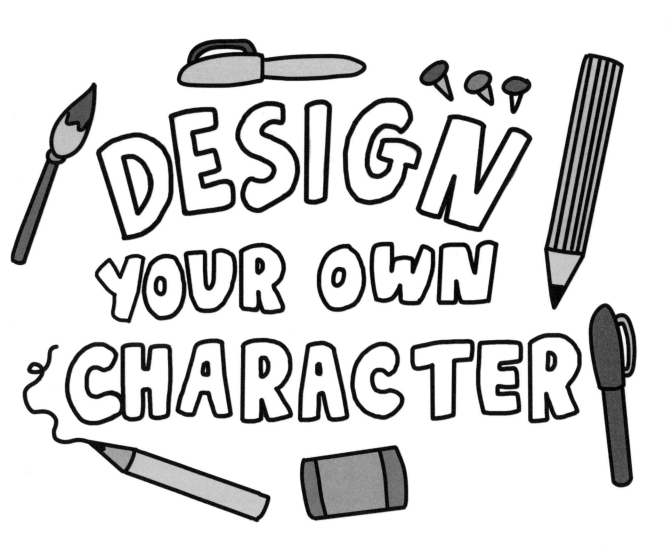

DESIGN YOUR OWN CHARACTER

When I grow up I would like to be a...

....

To do this...

I WILL:

- Believe in myself ☐
- Always do my best ☐
- Be kind ☐
- Look for ways to help other people ☐
- .... ☐

I CAN WORK HARDER IN:

- My maths lessons ☐
- My science lessons ☐
- My computing lessons ☐
- My art lessons ☐
- .... ☐

I CAN LEARN MORE ABOUT:

- New technologies ☐
- Space travel ☐
- The human body ☐
- The natural world ☐
- .... ☐

I CAN LEARN THIS BY:

- Reading more books ☐
- Asking more questions ☐
- Doing research on the internet ☐
- Watching tv programmes ☐
- .... ☐

Anything is possible

Do you like . . .

- [ ]
- [ ]
- [ ]

Follow the Maze

to find your way to an awesome career of the future

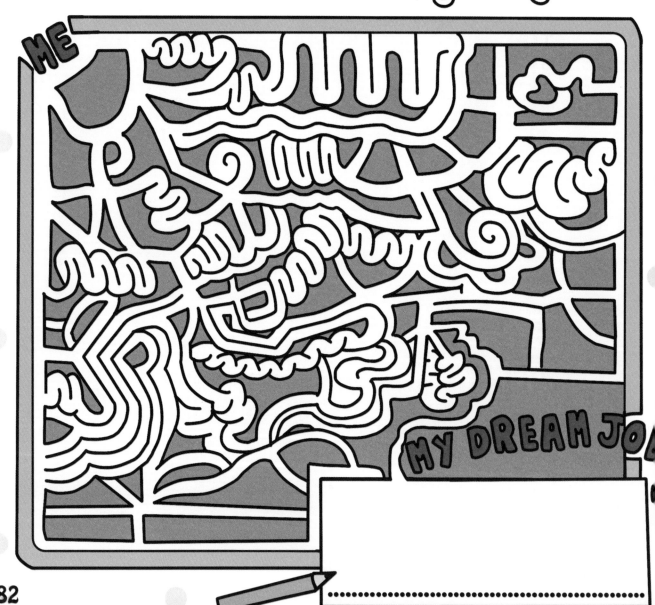

ME

MY DREAM JOB

WORDSEARCH

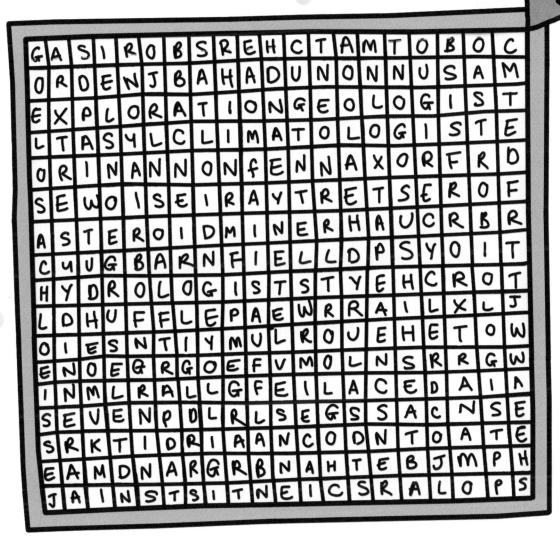

G	A	S	I	R	O	B	S	R	E	H	C	T	A	M	T	O	B	O	C
O	R	D	E	N	J	B	A	H	A	D	U	N	O	N	N	U	S	A	M
E	X	P	L	O	R	A	T	I	O	N	G	E	O	L	O	G	I	S	T
L	T	A	S	Y	L	C	L	I	M	A	T	O	L	O	G	I	S	T	E
O	R	I	N	A	N	N	O	N	F	E	N	N	A	X	O	R	F	R	D
S	E	W	O	I	S	E	I	R	A	Y	T	R	E	T	S	E	R	O	F
A	S	T	E	R	O	I	D	M	I	N	E	R	H	A	U	C	R	B	R
C	U	U	G	B	A	R	N	F	I	E	L	L	D	P	S	Y	O	I	T
H	Y	D	R	O	L	O	G	I	S	T	S	T	Y	E	H	C	R	O	T
L	D	H	U	F	F	L	E	P	A	E	W	R	R	A	I	L	X	L	J
O	I	E	S	N	T	I	Y	M	U	L	R	O	U	E	H	E	T	O	W
E	N	O	E	Q	R	G	O	E	F	V	M	O	L	N	S	R	R	G	W
I	N	M	L	R	A	L	L	G	F	E	I	L	A	C	E	D	A	I	A
S	E	V	E	N	P	D	L	R	L	S	E	G	S	S	A	C	N	S	E
S	R	K	T	I	D	R	I	A	A	N	C	O	D	N	T	O	A	T	E
E	A	M	D	N	A	R	G	R	B	N	A	H	T	E	B	J	M	P	H
J	A	I	N	S	T	S	I	T	N	E	I	C	S	R	A	L	O	P	S

Asteroid Miner
Space Nurse
Cobot Matcher
Exploration Geologist
Telesurgeon
Astrobiologist

Forester
Polar Scientist
Hydrologist
Climatologist
Diplomat
Recycler

Awesome Ideas

The world is full of awesome opportunities. Tick all the things you'd like to do one day:

- ○ - Learn a new language ☐
- - Travel to 20 different countries ☐
- - Swim all the way around an island ☐
- - Fly in a helicopter ☐
- - Swim with penguins ☐
- ○ - See gorillas in the wild ☐
- - Learn to surf ☐
- - Build an igloo ☐
- - Walk on a glacier ☐
- ○ - Snorkel over a coral reef ☐
- - Grow your own vegetables ☐

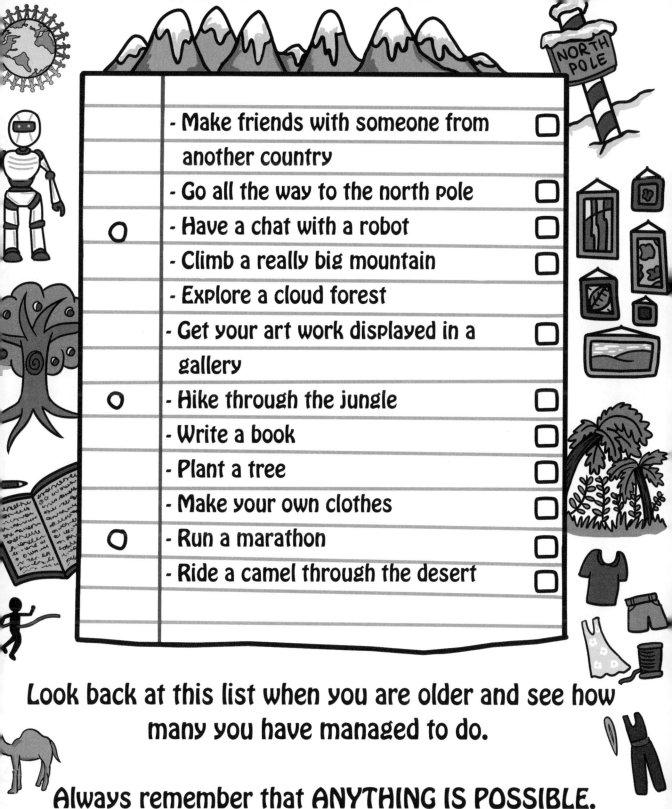

- Make friends with someone from another country ☐
- Go all the way to the north pole ☐
- Have a chat with a robot ☐
- Climb a really big mountain ☐
- Explore a cloud forest
- Get your art work displayed in a gallery ☐
- Hike through the jungle ☐
- Write a book ☐
- Plant a tree ☐
- Make your own clothes ☐
- Run a marathon ☐
- Ride a camel through the desert ☐

Look back at this list when you are older and see how many you have managed to do.

Always remember that **ANYTHING IS POSSIBLE.**

About the Author

Bryony Mathew is a British diplomat with a passion for inspiring children and showing them that everyone is equal. She has travelled all over the world, from Zambia, Indonesia and the Democratic Republic of Congo to Greenland, Brazil and the Philippines. Bryony has held diplomatic positions in India and China; most recently, she was deputy ambassador to Cambodia. She has a PhD in neuroscience, an MSc in primate brain evolution, is a mum of two, and likes to run.

About the Illustrator

Millie Bicknelle is a Creative Writer and Illustrator currently based in London. Nothing gives her greater pleasure than bringing a writer's idea to life, giving the most imaginative, detailed and accurate representation of the characters they enjoyed inventing so much. She has travelled around the world, working with children in Spain, Greece, Canada, and even as an elf for Santa in Lapland. With her love for children and her love for stories, she decided to combine the two together and come back to London to work on Children's Books full time.

For my Dad

Copyright © Bryony Mathew, 2019

First edition

Published in the United Kingdom in 2019

Edited by Katherine Mechling

Printed in Italy by L.E.G.O. S.p.A.

A CIP catalogue record for this book is available from the British Library.

ISBN: 978-1-9164515-3-7